Some words you will find in this book:

luach	לוּחַ	calendar
Machzor	מַחְזוֹר	festival prayer book
Rosh Hashanah	ראש הַשָּׁנָה	New Year
shalom	שָׁלוֹם	peace
Shanah Tovah	שָׁנָה טוֹבָה	Happy New Year
shofar	שׁוֹפָר	ram's horn
Torah	תּוֹרָה	scrolls of the Law

Acknowledgements

Some of the scenes in this book have been re-enacted to comply with Jewish tradition. The author and publishers would like to thank the Aronson family, Ron May, Miriam Kochan, and the President and members of the Oxford Jewish congregation – especially the children. Without their kindness and co-operation this book could not have been written.

The photograph on page 3 is reproduced with the permission of Susan Griggs; one photograph on page 4 (shofar blowing) is from the Rothschild Miscellany, North Italy, c. 1470, Courtesy of the Israel Museum; the other (shofarot) is reproduced with the permission of Pitt Rivers Museum, University of Oxford.

Design by Tony Garrett

First published in Great Britain 1987 by
Hamish Hamilton Children's Books
27 Wrights Lane, London W8 5TZ
Copyright © 1987 (text) by José Patterson
Copyright © 1987 (photographs) by Liba Taylor
All rights reserved

British Library Cataloguing in Publication Data
Patterson, José
    A happy new year.——(Way we live series).
    1. Rosh ha-Shanah——Juvenile literature
    I. Title   II. Series
    394.2'68296431'0941   BM695.N5

    ISBN 0-241-12047-0

Printed in Great Britain

A HAPPY NEW YEAR

José Patterson   Photographs by Liba Taylor

Hamish Hamilton   London

A New Year is not only celebrated on the first day of
January. The Jewish New Year begins in September or
October. It is celebrated on the first and second days of
Tishri, the seventh month in the Hebrew calendar.

Hebrew is the language of the Jews. It has twenty-two letters
and ten vowels, and is written from right to left. The letters
are written first; the vowels which look like dots and dashes,
are added afterwards. The New Year is called Rosh
Hashanah and it is written like this

רֹאשׁ הַשָּׁנָה

OCTOBER

ראשון SUN	שני MON	שלישי TUE	רביעי WED	חמישי THU	ששי FRI	שבת SAT
			1 כז	2 כח	3 כט	4 א Rosh Hashana 1st א' ראש השנה
5 בכ Rosh Hashana 2nd ב' ראש השנה	6 ג	7 ד	8 ה	9 ו	10 ז	11 ח
12 ט	13 י Yom Kippur יום כיפור	14 יא	15 יב	16 יג	17 יד	18 טו Succoth סוכות
19 טז	20 יז	21 יח	22 יט	23 כ	24 כא	25 כב Simhat Torah שמחת תורה
26 כג Simhat Torah	27 כד	28 כה	29 כו	30 כז	31 כח	

A Hebrew calendar is called a luach. Each Hebrew letter
stands for a number. Can you see Rosh Hashanah on the
calendar?

Although Jewish people live all over the world, many care
deeply about Israel, the land of the Bible. Jews there speak
Hebrew every day. Elsewhere it is used only in prayers.

In ancient times, Jews prayed in the Temple in Jerusalem.
(Jerusalem is the capital of Israel.) It was a large, beautiful
building. Since it was destroyed nearly two thousand years
ago, the Jews have mourned its loss. Today, all that remains
is the Western Wall where many Jews still pray.

Rosh Hashanah is a time to make a fresh start. Jews go to
the synagogue to ask God's forgiveness for their sins during
the past year, and pray that He will put their names in the
'Book of Life'. Very religious Jews ask their friends and
neighbours to forgive and forget any quarrels between them.
They use a festival prayer book called a Machzor.

This picture is from an old Machzor. It shows some people
listening to a man blowing a ram's horn, called a shofar.
The shofar has been blown on Rosh Hashanah for thousands
of years.

Here are some different kinds of shofar. They were used in synagogues in many parts of the world.

Ten days after Rosh Hashanah comes Yom Kippur, the Day of Atonement. This is the holiest day in the Jewish year. People think about the sins they have committed and pray for forgiveness. Grown-ups fast throughout the day.

This is Natalie and her brother Simon. Natalie is six years old and Simon is eight. They also have Hebrew names. Natalie's are Menucha Leah, and Simon's are Shimon Menachem. Jewish people often give their children well-known Bible names. Do you know which of Natalie's and Simon's names are from the Bible?

Simon is teaching Natalie to ride her bicycle.

'As soon as you can balance properly, we'll go for a ride with Mum and Dad,' he says.

The children's father is called Jeff. He is a doctor and works in a big hospital making medicines for sick people. When he gets home from work, he sometimes plays cricket with Simon and Natalie.

'This is how you hold the ball to get a good spin,' he explains.

Natalie is getting excited about Rosh Hashanah. This year she is being allowed to stay up for the festival meal. Last year she was too young. Natalie's mother, Renée, takes her shopping. They are going to buy Natalie a new dress to wear to the synagogue. They search and search until, at last, they find exactly what they want.

'Now let's go to the greengrocer,' says Renée. She wants to buy a fruit the family hasn't eaten during the year. If she finds one, they will eat it on the second day of the festival. A special blessing is said then to thank God for being able to enjoy new things. The blessing is called Shehechiyanu.

But although the greengrocer has many different fruits, they can't find anything new.

On Sunday mornings Simon and Natalie go to Hebrew classes. They learn to read and write Hebrew. They also learn about Jewish history, festivals and prayers. The boys each wear a little hat called a kipa. They cover their heads in this way as a sign of respect for God.

The children take turns to read from the Torah scroll. It contains the five books of Moses. The books describe how God gave his Law to the Jewish people more than three thousand years ago.

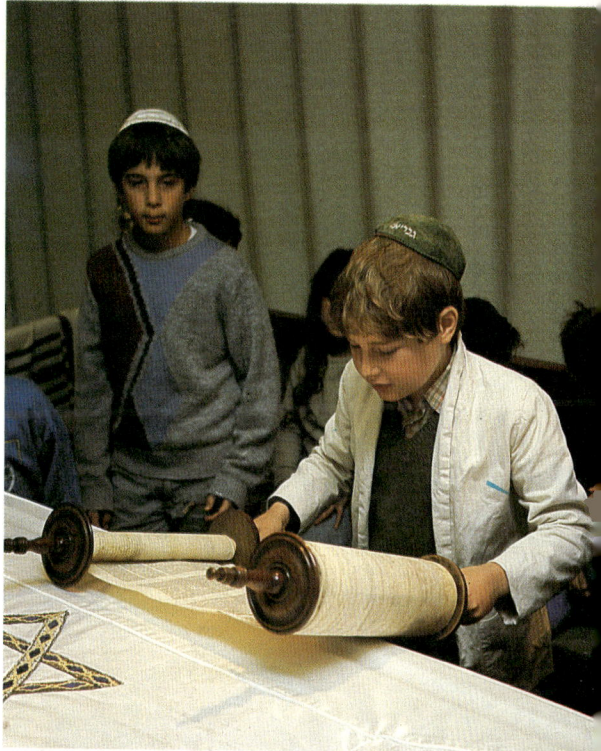

Simon tries to blow the shofar. But although he puffs very hard, no sound comes out.

'Let me have a go,' says Natalie.

Simon wears a special prayer shawl. It is called a tallit. Jewish boys and men wear a tallit during services in the synagogue.

At Rosh Hashanah, people send New Year cards to their family and friends. The cards say Shanah Tovah, a Happy New Year. This is how it is written:

שָׁנָה טוֹבָה

Natalie brings some New Year cards to show her class at school. Several of them have a picture of a seven-branched candlestick, called a menorah. A menorah was once used in the Temple in Jerusalem. One card has the word shalom written on it. This means 'peace'. It is also used for 'hello' and 'goodbye'.

Natalie carefully spreads honey on pieces of apple to give to the children. This is a New Year custom to wish everyone a sweet year. A special blessing for apple and honey will be said at the festival meal

Honey is also used for lekach, a honey cake baked specially for the New Year. Natalie pours some flour into a bowl.

'Stop!' says Mum, laughing. 'You've got to weigh it first.'

They decide to make two cakes, one to eat now and one for the festival.

'This is delicious,' says Simon.

'Better hide the other cake, or there won't be anything left for Rosh Hashanah,' Jeff says.

Kreplach are another traditional festival food. Bobba, Natalie's grandmother, shows her how to make the dough from eggs, flour and water. Natalie rolls it out and cuts it into squares. A spoonful of cooked minced kosher meat is put on each square. (Food which Jews are allowed to eat is called kosher.) Then Natalie folds the squares into triangles and presses together the two points on the folded edge. When the kreplach are cooked, they will be dropped into soup.

On the morning of the festival, the family goes to the synagogue. When they arrive, Jeff and Simon put on their tallit and kipa and sit down with the other men. Men and women sit separately in this synagogue.

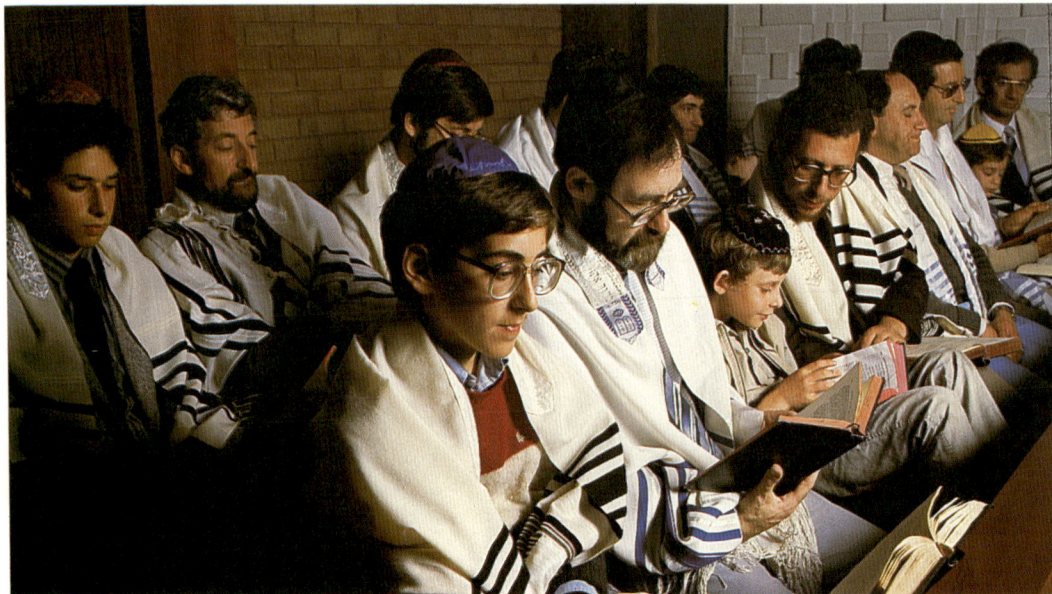

The Torah scrolls are kept inside the Aron Kodesh, the Holy Ark. They are wrapped in white embroidered covers for Rosh Hashanah. The Ark faces East, in the direction of Jerusalem. When the Ark is open, the congregation stands to say a special prayer. It is an honour to be asked to open and close the doors of the Ark.

At various times during the service, a man stands up to blow the shofar. It sounds a bit like a trumpet. The man plays a group of long and short notes by blowing hard and changing the position of his tongue. There are no finger holes on the shofar. Everyone stands to hear the shofar and to pray. This time, the sound is loud and clear.

The Torah scrolls are made of sheets of parchment sewn together with special thread. The Hebrew words are written by hand. A man called a scribe uses a goose feather quill pen to write them. He cuts the nib with a very sharp knife. It takes more than a year to write one Torah scroll.

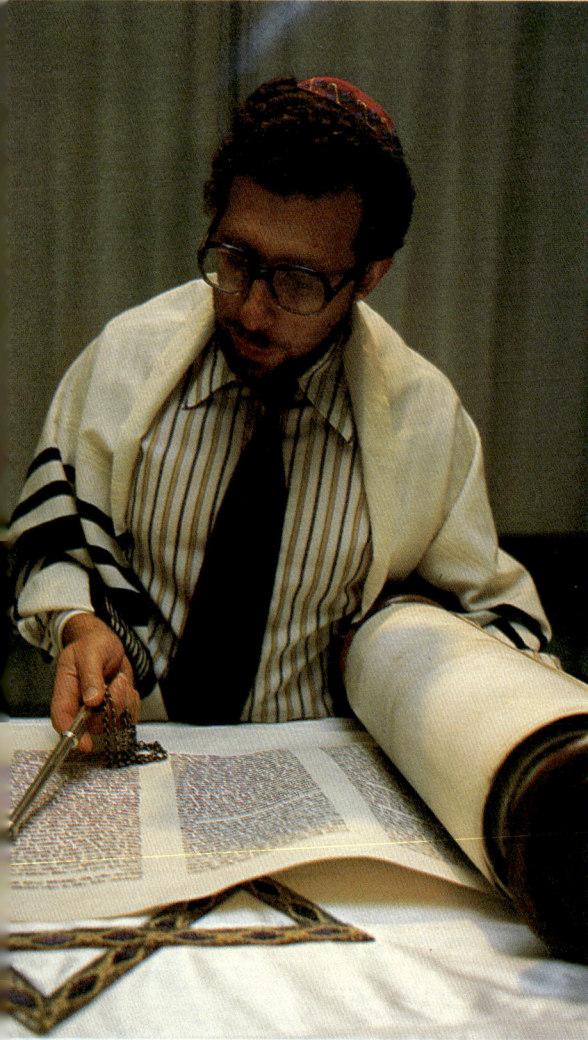

The service is led by the chazan, who chants the prayers. Jeff is 'called up' to read from the Torah. The chazan calls him by his Hebrew names, Yoseph Kalman ben Shmuel (Joseph Kalman son of Samuel). He is proud to be asked, especially as it is Rosh Hashanah. He uses a pointer, called a yad, to help him keep his place. Fingers are not allowed.

Torah readings are divided into portions. When the last portion has been read, the Torah is held up for everyone to see.

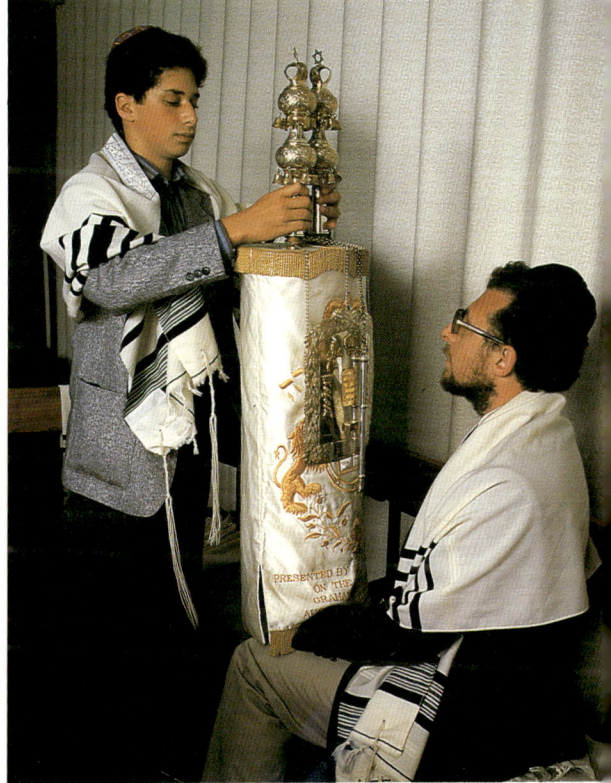

The scroll is covered and silver ornaments are put over the handles. The tiny bells ring when the Torah is carried back to the Ark. Everyone sits down and the rabbi (minister) preaches a sermon.

After the service is over, people greet their friends and wish
them Shanah Tovah – a Happy New Year. Everyone is
cheerful. Back at home, there is a surprise for Natalie. Renée
gives her a pomegranate.

'It comes from Israel,' she says. 'We'll eat it for the New
Year blessing.'

'Oooh, lovely,' says Natalie. 'I haven't tasted
pomegranate before.'

Later that afternoon Renée's parents, Bobba and Zaideh, arrive. Normally, all four grandparents join the family to celebrate together, but this year Jeff's mother is too ill to travel. Natalie takes Bobba upstairs to show her the new dress. Natalie is going to wear it tonight.

'You will look pretty,' says Bobba.

But first, Natalie and Simon must help lay the table. It takes a long time. When they have finished, Bobba and Zaideh come to admire it.

'How beautiful it looks,' says Zaideh.

Soon afterwards, some friends arrive for dinner. Everyone gathers round the table and Jeff says a prayer over the kosher wine. Then Jeff blesses the bread. This kind of bread is called challah. It is made into two plaited loaves for every Sabbath, but for the New Year it is baked into a special round shape. Jeff cuts everyone a slice.

A plate with slices of apple and a pot of honey is passed around. Each person takes one slice, and dips a piece of bread into the honey.

'I wish you a sweet year,' says Natalie.

The pomegranate is cut up and Jeff reads the Shehechiyanu prayer. The red seeds are sweet and juicy – a lovely new taste.

When the blessings have been read, Renée serves dinner. They are having roast chicken, green beans, roast potatoes, apple pie and honey cake. But first there is chicken soup, with Natalie's kreplach floating in it. Everyone says they are delicious.

The meal lasts a long time. By the end, Simon and Natalie are ready for bed. It has been a lovely day, although the children are sad that Grandma and Grandad couldn't be with them. Bobba gives Natalie a big goodnight hug.

'Shanah Tovah,' she says, 'Happy New Year.'

Natalie's lekach

You will need

8oz (200g) plain flour
8oz (200g) clear honey
4oz (100g) caster sugar
½ teaspoon ginger
½ teaspoon cinnamon
½ teaspoon mixed spice
1 teaspoon bicarbonate of soda
2 eggs
4 fluid oz (100ml) cooking oil
4 fluid oz (100ml) orange juice

1 bowl, 1 sieve, 1 wooden spoon, 1 teaspoon, 1 shallow cake tin, lined with greaseproof paper, 1 wire rack

1. Sieve the flour and mixed spice, ginger and cinammon into a bowl. Add the sugar.
2. Make a dip in the middle. Add the honey, oil and beaten eggs.
3. Beat very well with the wooden spoon.
4. Stir the bicarbonate of soda into the orange juice. Add the juice to the cake mixture.
5. Pour the mixture into the tin.
6. Bake for 1½ hours at gas mark 3 (325°F, 170°C). Ask an adult to put the tin into the oven, and take it out for you.
7. Turn the cake out of the tin and leave it to cool on the wire rack. Wrap the cake in foil and store in a cake tin for a few days – if you can resist it! It tastes much better this way.